Travel To...
PLACES OF
PROTEST

Jen Breach

Rourke
Educational Media

A Division of
Carson
Dellosa
Education

BEFORE AND DURING READING ACTIVITIES

Before Reading: *Building Background Knowledge and Vocabulary*

Building background knowledge can help children process new information and build upon what they already know. Before reading a book, it is important to tap into what children already know about the topic. This will help them develop their vocabulary and increase their reading comprehension.

Questions and Activities to Build Background Knowledge:

1. Look at the front cover of the book and read the title. What do you think this book will be about?
2. What do you already know about this topic?
3. Take a book walk and skim the pages. Look at the table of contents, photographs, captions, and bold words. Did these text features give you any information or predictions about what you will read in this book?

Vocabulary: *Vocabulary Is Key to Reading Comprehension*

Use the following directions to prompt a conversation about each word.

- Read the vocabulary words.
- What comes to mind when you see each word?
- What do you think each word means?

Vocabulary Words:
- annexed
- autocratic
- avant-garde
- delegation
- federal
- genocide
- LGBTQ+
- patriarch
- protesters
- provocative
- reconciliation
- taboos

During Reading: *Reading for Meaning and Understanding*

To achieve deep comprehension of a book, children are encouraged to use close reading strategies. During reading, it is important to have children stop and make connections. These connections result in deeper analysis and understanding of a book.

 Close Reading a Text

During reading, have children stop and talk about the following:

- Any confusing parts
- Any unknown words
- Text to text, text to self, text to world connections
- The main idea in each chapter or heading

Encourage children to use context clues to determine the meaning of any unknown words. These strategies will help children learn to analyze the text more thoroughly as they read.

When you are finished reading this book, turn to page 46 for **Text-Dependent Questions** and an **Extension Activity**.

TABLE of CONTENTS

SITTING IN SAN FRANCISCO

THE FEDERAL BUILDING

50 UNITED NATIONS PLAZA

SAN FRANCISCO

San Francisco is known as the Rainbow City for its colorfully painted houses and as the origin of the Gay Pride flag. But its Civic Center is much like civic centers elsewhere: large, gray, important-looking stone buildings housing government offices. The Civic Center at 50 United Nations Plaza looks almost the same today as it did in 1977, when more than 100 people with disabilities, plus their allies, moved in for a sit-in that lasted 25 days called the 504 Sit-in.

The Federal Building, 50 United Nations Plaza

A sit-in is a form of nonviolent protest where people occupy a space, usually public or governmental, to pressure an authority to meet their demands. The **protesters** in the 504 Sit-in demanded that a law protecting the rights of people with disabilities be put into action. Beyond medical needs, there was very little **federal** assistance granted to people with disabilities. Even though schools, libraries, transportation, and more were made available to the public, that didn't mean people with disabilities were able to access them. Section 504 of the Rehabilitation Act of 1973 changed that.

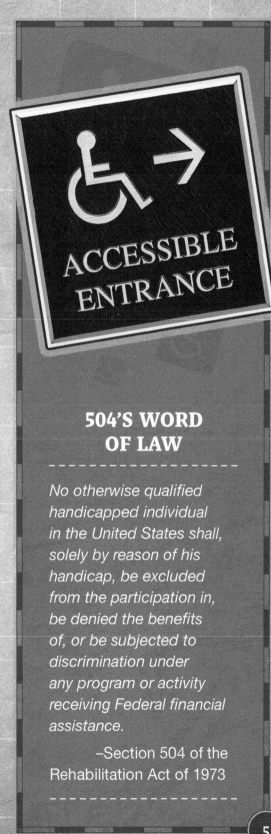

504'S WORD OF LAW

- - - - - - - - - - - - - - - - - -

No otherwise qualified handicapped individual in the United States shall, solely by reason of his handicap, be excluded from the participation in, be denied the benefits of, or be subjected to discrimination under any program or activity receiving Federal financial assistance.

–Section 504 of the Rehabilitation Act of 1973

- - - - - - - - - - - - - - - - - -

Kitty Cone was a disability rights activist and one of the leaders of the 504 Sit-in.

After the Rehabilitation Act was passed, Americans with disabilities and their allies waited for the regulations that would change their lives to be put into action…

and waited… for more than four years.

The regulations were written, but the Department of Health, Education, and Welfare (HEW) was delaying their release. The regulations were going to be costly. Incoming President Jimmy Carter wanted to weaken the regulations, reducing their impact. The newly formed American Coalition of Citizens with Disabilities (ACCD) demanded that the regulations be released by April 4th, 1977, or they would take action on April 5.

The regulations were not released.

On April 5, ACCD members decided that if they were being forced to wait, they would wait in a place where no one could ignore them. They met no resistance from building security as they moved into the HEW regional offices on the fourth floor of 50 United Nations Plaza in San Francisco, California. Demonstrations were also held in front of HEW offices in Atlanta, Boston, Chicago, Dallas, Denver, Philadelphia, New York, and Seattle, and at the HEW headquarters in Washington, D.C.

The San Francisco sit-in was grueling for the protesters, many of whom had very specific physical needs. ACCD members outside the building made sure that the protesters had access to mattresses, their medications, and meals. They also kept the press involved. The protesters endured false bomb threats and other attempts from law enforcement to flush them out of the building.

Eventually, 22 members of the sit-in were sent to Washington, D.C., to address President Carter, the HEW Secretary, and other politicians. Even though they were exhausted from weeks of protesting, the **delegation** took dozens of meetings. They calmly rebuffed arguments to weaken the 504 regulations and changed the hearts and minds of many lawmakers.

The protesters' efforts made an impact. A full 23 days after the sit-in began, the regulations were signed and released, unchanged. The protest was a success! While Section 504 only applied to federal jobs, schools, services, and programs, it was an important start for what would come later. In 1990, the Americans with Disabilities Act (ADA) passed. This act encompassed all public spaces and private institutions and workplaces. People with disabilities finally had access to every part of everyday life.

Evan Kemp, Chairman of the Equal Employment Opportunity Commission, looks on as President George H. W. Bush signs the ADA of 1990 into law.

OPEN DOORS NEED RAMPS

President Carter liked to call his administration the "Open Door Administration," meaning that anyone had access to members of his government at any time. The ACCD Washington, D.C. delegation followed Carter to buildings where he held speeches and meetings, most of which were inaccessible in a wheelchair. The delegation demonstrated that an open door didn't matter if people couldn't get up the stairs.

THE CATHEDRAL OF
CHRIST THE SAVIOR
MOSCOW, RUSSIA

Patriarch Kirill

Russian President
Vladimir Putin

The Cathedral of Christ the Savior is the headquarters of the Russian Orthodox Church in Moscow, Russia. It is a strikingly beautiful church—tall, shimmering white, and gold domed. For Pussy Riot, a punk music group formed by 11 female activists, the cathedral was the perfect place to criticize the head of the Russian Orthodox Church, **Patriarch** Kirill, and Russian President Vladimir Putin. In 2012, the patriarch had campaigned on behalf of Putin who Pussy Riot saw as corrupt and **autocratic**. The patriarch and the church are supposed to be politically independent and not support any particular party or candidate.

In February 2012, the Russian presidential election was just weeks away. Putin was certain to win for the third time, despite increased public protest. Patriarch Kirill publicly supported Putin and urged all Russian Orthodox people to vote for him. Many people, including Pussy Riot, felt that the church's backing of a corrupt politician made the church corrupt, too.

In response, the band recorded a "punk prayer" protest song as a piece of guerilla art. Guerilla art is a form of protest, usually nonviolent and often involving humor, that involves unofficial or unapproved art in a public space that has a political or social message. The song combined prayers with their regular punk style. Pussy Riot's song also referenced the rights of women and **LGBTQ+** people, who are regularly oppressed in Russia.

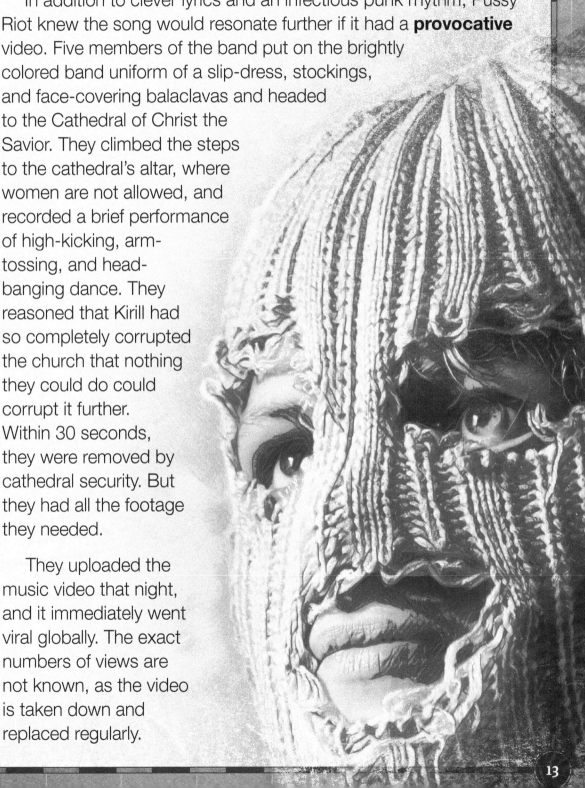

In addition to clever lyrics and an infectious punk rhythm, Pussy Riot knew the song would resonate further if it had a **provocative** video. Five members of the band put on the brightly colored band uniform of a slip-dress, stockings, and face-covering balaclavas and headed to the Cathedral of Christ the Savior. They climbed the steps to the cathedral's altar, where women are not allowed, and recorded a brief performance of high-kicking, arm-tossing, and head-banging dance. They reasoned that Kirill had so completely corrupted the church that nothing they could do could corrupt it further. Within 30 seconds, they were removed by cathedral security. But they had all the footage they needed.

They uploaded the music video that night, and it immediately went viral globally. The exact numbers of views are not known, as the video is taken down and replaced regularly.

Pussy Riot member Maria Alyokhina is detained by police.

Soon, three members of the band—Nadezhda Tolokonnikova, Yekaterina Samutsevich, and Maria Alyokhina—were identified and charged with "hooliganism," a type of disorderly conduct considered to be motivated by religious hatred. The remaining group members fled the country or went into hiding.

The trial was covered by Western media and sparked further protests in Russia. All three Pussy Riot members were found guilty and two served nearly two years in a Russian prison. Putin is still the president of Russia, and he is still openly supported by Patriarch Kirill. The three members of Pussy Riot who were imprisoned were all released, and the band continues their activism.

WORLD CUP (PUSSY) RIOT

The 2018 FIFA World Cup was held in Moscow. The final was watched by more than a billion people on television. It was a perfect stage for a Pussy Riot protest. Four group members dressed as Russian police officers and invaded the pitch, stopping play for about 30 seconds. The action highlighted the unquestioned authority of a police uniform in Russia – the activists were never asked to show identification as they were ushered through several security checkpoints on their way to the pitch. In a video posted later, Pussy Riot called for more transparency and less brutality in Russian policing, and for open political competition.

UNREST IN FERGUSON

FERGUSON

MISSOURI

HANDS UP, DON'T SHOOT

HANDS UP, DON'T SHOOT

Rest In Power

MIKE BROWN

Michael Brown

BLACK LIVES MATTE

Ferguson is a small city on the suburban edge of St. Louis, Missouri. Three key things set Ferguson apart from other places in the country. First, of its roughly 20,000 residents, 67% are Black, compared to the 13% Black population of the country. Second, its police force is 90% white. And most importantly, it is where a white police officer shot and killed an 18-year-old unarmed Black man named Michael Brown on August 9, 2014.

Over the following weeks, members of the Black community and their allies faced off against law enforcement again and again, illustrating the countrywide tension between police and Black communities. Many of the demonstrators were peaceful, gathering to sing or marching and chanting "Hands up! Don't shoot!" and "Black Lives Matter." But some people expressed their anger and frustration through rioting. Rioting is a kind of protest that involves a group behaving violently, often involving weapons and the destruction of property. The rioters in Ferguson threw rocks and bottles and damaged several businesses and vehicles through arson and looting. Some were surprised and disappointed that there were protesters who became destructive and violent. Others felt that the urgency of the protesters' message, compounded by years of systemic racism in law enforcement practices, warranted this method of protest.

In response, Ferguson city police showed up in body armor and Kevlar helmets with shields, rubber bullets, tear gas canisters, and canine units.

Over the following days and nights of protests and riots, police numbers were reinforced by law enforcement from surrounding towns, state troopers, Missouri SWAT teams, and the Missouri National Guard. The addition of the SWAT team units and the National Guard brought a militaristic edge to the force. They came equipped with camouflage uniforms, armored tactical vehicles, sharpshooters, and military-grade weapons. News media reports corroborated the civilian social media reports of police using excessive force against rioters, peaceful protesters, and the media alike. By the third night of protests and riots, the police had arrested more than 400 people.

President Barack Obama, giving a brief speech from Edgerton, Massachusetts, said "There's also no excuse for police to use excessive force against peaceful protests, or to throw protesters in jail for lawfully exercising their First Amendment rights. And here, in the United States of America, police should not be bullying or arresting journalists who are just trying to do their jobs and report to the American people on what they see on the ground."

President Barack Obama

Hundreds gathered at the site where Michael Brown was shot.

The use of excessive force by law enforcement contributed to increased tension, frustration, and weeks of violence in Ferguson, the ripples of which are still being felt. In 2015, a U.S. Department of Justice investigation into Ferguson city police found that their practices frequently broke the law and damaged the community trust, especially among Black people. Ferguson police were found to routinely violate the civil rights of Black citizens, which became the tinderbox for the Ferguson riots, struck by the match of Michael Brown's murder.

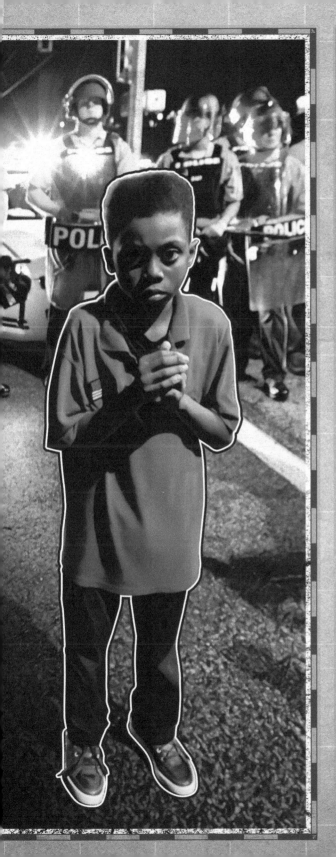

BLACK LIVES MATTER

An important modern social justice movement founded in 2013, Black Lives Matter works in communities and online to fight racism and white supremacy. They focus on police brutality, which is far more likely to be experienced by people of color than white people, and the murder of Black people by law enforcement. Common #BLM or #BlackLivesMatter responses are large-scale street demonstrations and social media campaigns. They were also active in promoting Juneteenth as a national holiday to center and celebrate Black history as U.S. history.

MARCHING IN SYDNEY

SYDNEY HARBOUR BRIDGE
SYDNEY, AUSTRALIA

When most people think of Sydney, Australia, they probably picture the glinting white sails of the Sydney Opera House and the Sydney Harbour Bridge spanning sparkling blue water. It's an iconic image, which is exactly why it was chosen for the 2000 "Walk for **Reconciliation**," a symbolic march for reconciliation between Aboriginal and Torres Strait Islander peoples and non-Indigenous Australians. Aboriginal Australians are the many Indigenous people of that continent. The Torres Strait Islanders are those people indigenous to the Torres Strait Islands north of the continent.

The Walk for Reconciliation at Sydney Harbour Bridge was scheduled for May 28, 2000. The date was as symbolic as the location. On the same day in 1997, a politically independent National Inquiry released a report on their findings on the extent and impact of the removing, sometimes forcibly, of Aboriginal and Torres Strait Islander children from their families between 1910 and 1970. The removed children were supposed to assimilate into white, colonial culture. These children are known as the "Stolen Generations."

The report stated that this removal of children was a gross violation of human rights and an act of **genocide**. The intention was to wipe out the Indigenous people and their cultures. Aboriginal and Torres Strait Islander people, who comprise 3% of the Australian population, are significantly more likely to experience joblessness, homelessness, health issues, prison, and discrimination than other Australians. The report included recommendations to improve their quality of life and to preserve their cultures. The report also urged Australia's Prime Minister, John Howard, to formally apologize on behalf of the Australian government (which has historically been almost exclusively white). Howard rejected the request to apologize as a "black armband view of history," meaning that the finding was an overly bleak view of Australia's past.

Prime Minister
John Howard

Sydney Harbour Bridge

Before the Reconciliation Walk, organizers were expecting that perhaps a few hundred would attend. In fact, between 200,000 and 300,000 people streamed across the bridge for nearly six hours. Organized walks in main cities across the country followed, including the Melbourne walk, where more than 300,000 people participated, protesting the lack of apology and advocating for racial equity.

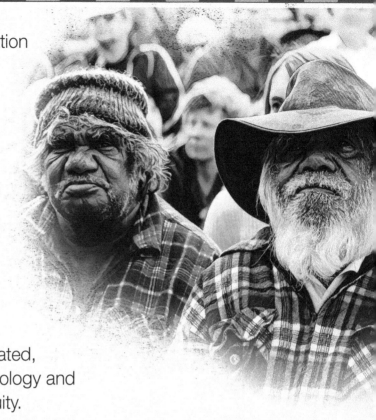

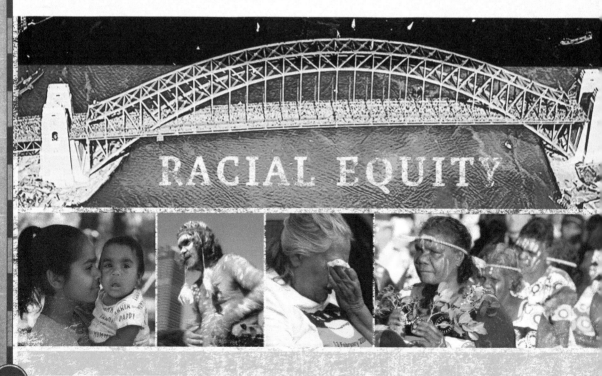

RACIAL EQUITY

A crowd looks on as Prime Minister Kevin Rudd apologizes to the Aboriginal and Torres Strait Islander people.

Sorry Day

NATIONAL DAY OF HEALING

"Commemoration for the Stolen Generations"

What is Sorry Day / National D...

This day, 26th May, offers the ...rtu
to acknowledge the human ... m...
th...n 150 years, of forcible ... ...nd
Torres Strait Islander chil...

THE AWAITED APOLOGY

The National Inquiry report called for a formal apology from the Australian government. Aboriginal and Torres Strait Islander people waited eight years until Prime Minister Kevin Rudd took office, succeeding John Howard, in 2008. The protests finally found success. Rudd's first Act of Parliament was an apology on behalf of the Australian Parliament to the Aboriginal and Torres Strait Islander people.

REVOLTING IN SIDI BOUZID

SIDI BOUZID

TUNISIA

Tunisia is a popular vacation destination for Europeans, especially the coasts where white and blue painted buildings overlook beaches on the sparkling Mediterranean Sea. Life in the interior, in places like Sidi Bouzid, is much more difficult. In 2010, unemployment was high, living conditions were poor, and food was expensive. A corrupt government turned a blind eye to these problems, which had been unchanged for a number of years. Many Tunisians, especially young people, were growing increasingly frustrated.

Tensions had been high for a while when they finally exploded after one man, Mohamed Bouazizi, made an act of protest. Bouazizi was 26 years old, lived in Sidi Bouzid, and supported his family of eight by selling fruit and vegetables from a cart. On December 17, 2010, a police officer confiscated Bouazizi's produce, claiming he did not have the necessary permits. Bouazizi attempted to register complaints with the government but went unheard. Now desperate and without hope, Bouazizi set himself on fire in front of the governor's office.

Sidi Bouzid

Mohamed Bouazizi

The story of Bouazizi's act of protest was the catalyst for the 28 days of protest that followed, spreading from his small town to all corners of the country and into the wider Arab world. That night, hundreds of students and young people gathered in front of the Sidi Bouzid local government offices to protest.

The Tunisian media suppressed coverage of the protests, especially in the first few days. But protesters used smartphones and other devices to capture footage of demonstrating, rioting, and police violence. These videos, posted to social media sites, soon prompted protests in other Tunisian cities and caught the attention of the international media and human rights watch groups. Social media turned what would have earlier been a local protest movement into a global phenomenon.

Tunisian protesters clash with security.

Every day and night for 28 days, Tunisian streets and public squares were crowded with demonstrators calling for fair, democratic elections and for President Zine el-Abidine Ben Ali to resign. Protesters clashed again and again with police who used riot gear, tear gas, and live ammunition.

Finally, on January 14, after 23 years in power, Ben Ali fled the country. Over 300 people had died, and thousands had been injured, but Tunisia held its first transparent democratic election in October that year.

Ben Ali

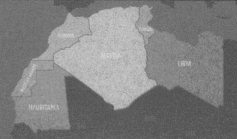

ARAB SPRING

The economic and political conditions in Tunisia were common in much of North Africa and the Arab world. After the Tunisian Revolution, protesters with the same simmering frustration over undemocratic rule, government oppression, and poor living conditions took to the streets and to social media in Egypt, Morocco, Oman, Palestine, Jordan, Bahrain, Kuwait, Algeria, and Lebanon. Armed rebellion shook Syria, Iraq, Libya, and Yemen. By the end of 2012, four governments had been overthrown, another six had been significantly altered, four civil wars had broken out, and more than 61,000 people had been killed. The region would never be the same again.

DRIVING IN RIYADH

RIYADH

SAUDI ARABIA

Riyadh, the capital of Saudi Arabia, is a city built on a desert. The light is harsh, the sun is hot, there is very little rain, and the air is often hazy with sandstorm pollution. In 1990, Riyadh was a tense and dangerous place. Under Saddam Hussein, neighboring Iraq had just **annexed** Kuwait, and much of the world feared that Saudi Arabia would be next. British and U.S. troops were deployed into Saudi Arabia, and the Gulf War began.

Among this uncertainty, rapid change, and tension, 47 women drove cars in a convoy through the city for around 30 minutes. It was a radical and provocative act of civil disobedience, protesting the kingdom's systemic oppression of women. Civil disobedience is a form of protest, usually nonviolent, where protesters intentionally break a law that they are campaigning to change.

Saudi Arabia's legal system is based on a strict interpretation of their holy book, the Koran. Some of the laws that come about because of this place severe limitations on the freedom of women. These laws dictate that men and women must be kept separate in public places, that women must be covered head to toe, and that women require the permission of a guardian (always male, usually a relative or husband) to obtain a passport, get a job, or even be released from prison. These laws are often based on widely understood social **taboos** that, in 1990, included a belief that women should not be allowed to drive. In the World Economic Forum 2021 Global Gender Gap report, Saudi Arabia was ranked 147 out of 156 countries for gender equality.

In 2011, Azza Al Shmasani drove in defiance of the ban on female drivers.

Over 20 years after this protest, in 2011, Saudi women's rights activist Manal al-Sharif wrote in the UK's *Guardian* newspaper that by driving, women could "stand up to repression, authoritarianism and tradition. We [were] pushing back against one of Saudi Arabia's most enduring cultural taboos."

A woman drives herself to work the day after the driving ban was lifted.

Protests and demonstrations are not always successful in bringing about change. In 1990, the women were arrested, their passports were confiscated, and those with jobs lost them. Their names, addresses, and phone numbers were published, and death threats soon followed. An official statement was issued saying that allowing women to drive could bring about "social chaos." Women driving was now not only culturally taboo, but utterly illegal.

The law stood for 28 years until it was overturned in 2018. Saudi Arabia was the last country in the world to allow women to drive.

Manal al-Sharif

UPRISING IN NEW YORK CITY

STONEWALL INN

NEW YORK CITY, NEW YORK

New York's Greenwich Village was once known as a haven for **avant-garde** artists, activists, and others outside of mainstream culture. It is home to the first racially integrated night club, and it was known as a place to embrace the radical and experimental that was otherwise ignored by contemporary arts and cultural establishments. The buildings were run down, organized crime was typical, and police raids were common. One such raid on the Stonewall Inn in 1969 became a pivotal moment in the modern fight for LGBTQ+ rights.

At the time, homosexuality was illegal in almost every state in the U.S. Bars known to serve LGBTQ+ people were frequently denied liquor licenses. Most gay bars, including the Stonewall Inn, were run by organized crime. They would pay off police in order to serve alcohol without a license. Raids on gay bars occurred about once a month. Police misconduct was common, including inappropriately touching, clubbing, punching, and kicking. People were arrested if they wore clothing that didn't match their assigned gender. After a raid, people who were allowed to leave generally scattered quickly, grateful that they were not arrested. Business in the bar usually resumed within hours as soon as any confiscated alcohol could be restocked.

Wearing clothing that did not match your assigned gender could lead to being arrested and charged with impersonation.

During June of 1969, raids became more frequent, and the bars were not always tipped off. At 1:20 a.m. on Saturday, June 28, 1969, members of the Public Morals Squad of the New York Police Department arrived at the Stonewall Inn undercover, finding over 200 patrons in the hot, cramped bar.

Reports vary about exact events on June 28, but it's clear that once the police raided the bar, the patrons who were allowed to leave did not scatter as usual but stayed on the street and sidewalk outside the Stonewall Inn. They clapped and cheered for the people being arrested and moved into police wagons, showing them their support.

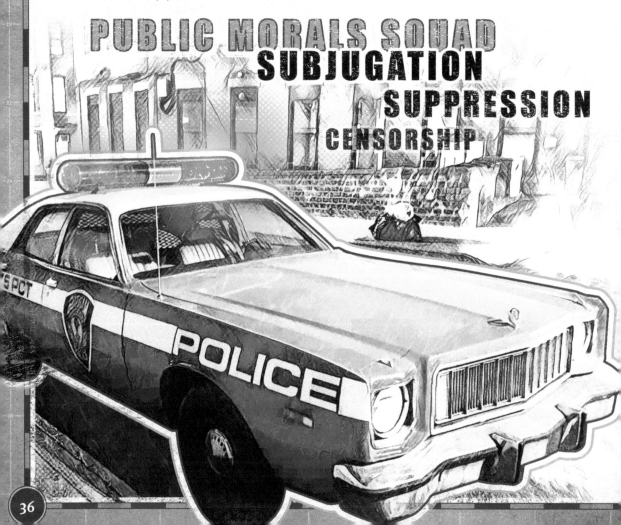

PUBLIC MORALS SQUAD
SUBJUGATION
SUPPRESSION
CENSORSHIP

The Stonewall Inn

The events that began at the Stonewall Inn in 1969 marked a monumental change for lesbian, gay, bisexual, transgender and queer (LGBTQ) Americans. Stonewall, which occupied 51-53 Christopher Street, was a gay bar that was raided on June 28, 1969. Patrons and a crowd outside resisted, and confrontations continued over the next few nights in nearby Christopher Park and on adjacent streets. This uprising catalyzed the LGBTQ civil rights movement, resulting in increased visibility for the community that continues to resonate in the struggle for equality.

New York State Historic Site
2016

When a handcuffed woman was hit in the head by a police officer as she was being taken to the wagon, the crowd responded. The most vocal and active protesters were the young and homeless LGBTQ+ people who considered the Stonewall Inn and other gay bars to be their only safe space.

A REFLECTION ON A SPONTANEOUS MOMENT

"We all had a collective feeling like we'd had enough of this kind of [thing]. It wasn't anything tangible anybody said to anyone else, it was just kind of like everything over the years had come to a head on that one particular night in the one particular place… All kinds of people, all different reasons, but mostly it was total outrage, anger, sorrow, everything combined. [We stood our] ground for the first time… There was something in the air, freedom a long time overdue and we're going to fight for it."

– Stonewall rioter Michel Fader, recorded by historian David Carter in 2004

The crowd, which grew in number to over 400 as people were attracted by singing and chanting, threw coins and bottles at the police, who had barricaded inside the Stonewall Inn while waiting for reinforcements. The bar was set on fire.

The following night, the Stonewall Inn, though almost destroyed inside, declared in graffiti "We Are Open." Thousands of people—LGBTQ+ people who had or had not been there the night before, allies, students, and other locals—gathered on the street outside the bar, while about 100 police officers struggled to control the crowd. Skirmishes broke out and a few people were arrested. Protests and arrests continued for the next few days as LGBTQ+ people and their allies faced off against police.

The Stonewall Uprising was not the first event in LGBTQ+ activism, but it was a crucial moment. In the following months, a number of activist groups were founded that contributed significantly over the following decades to LGBTQ+ rights advocacy. The anniversary of the Stonewall Uprising is marked annually in New York City with a gay pride parade: the first anniversary was the first gay pride parade the city ever held. The 50th anniversary, in 2019, was the largest pride parade in history, with more than five million people marching from Greenwich Village to Central Park.

Members of the Gay Officers Action League (GOAL)

WALKING OUT IN PARKLAND

MARJORY STONEMAN DOUGLAS HIGH SCHOOL

PARKLAND, FLORIDA

Parkland, Florida, is a leafy, affluent suburb of humid Miami. Prior to 2018, it was one of the safest towns in Florida. But on February 14, 2018, a 19-year-old former student of Marjory Stoneman Douglas High School brought legally purchased assault rifles onto campus, murdering 17 people. It was the worst high school shooting in American history.

Police assist in evacuating students from Marjory Stoneman Douglas High School after the shooting.

Days of rallies, vigils, and gatherings followed—collective experiences of disbelief and grief from students, parents, teachers, and community members. But there was also anger and calls to action on gun control. At a rally on February 17, survivor of the shooting X González said "the people in the government who are voted into power are lying to us. And us kids seem to be the only ones who notice and are prepared to call BS."

One month later, on March 14 at 10:00 a.m., about 3,000 students of Marjory Stoneman Douglas High School and most of the faculty and staff walked out of class and gathered on the school's sports field. A walkout is a peaceful protest in which a group collectively agrees to stop work. The demonstration lasted 17 minutes, symbolic of the 17 victims of the February 14 shooting.

MARJORY STONEMAN DOUGLAS

NOT JUST A NAMESAKE

- -

Marjory Stoneman Douglas (1890-1998) was an American journalist and lifelong activist. She is best known as the "Dame of the Everglades" for her conservationist work to save Florida's wetlands from drainage and development. In 1980, she wrote: "Be a nuisance when it counts. Do your part to inform and stimulate the public to join your action. Be depressed, discouraged, and disappointed at failure and the disheartening effects of ignorance, greed, corruption & bad politics—but never give up."

- -

At the same time, students, parents, and teachers in nearly 3,100 schools across the country were doing the same. In Washington, D.C., thousands of students and their allies observed 17 minutes of silence with their backs to the White House. The national demonstration was organized through social media channels using hashtags #NeverAgain and #EnoughIsEnough. It encouraged the use of the walkout to highlight the violence they were protesting. This walkout marked the beginning of the student-led movement for gun control in the U.S.

Following such a huge show of support for gun control, student activists demanded action from lawmakers. Lawmakers were quick in some places to raise the legal age for buying assault rifles to 21 and ban bump stocks, which allow semi-automatic weapons to fire faster, and other paraphernalia that has contributed to mass killings. But arguments continue from pro-gun groups that school shootings and other murder sprees are more an issue of mental health than they are of gun control. The National Rifle Association (NRA) redoubled its insistence that more guns is the answer to stopping mass shootings, not less. The NRA also advocates for arming schoolteachers in classrooms.

Marjory Stoneman Douglas High School was not the last school shooting in the U.S. – just three months later 10 were killed and 13 injured at Santa Fe High School in Texas. Nevertheless, student activism continues for greater gun control.

WE TRAVELED TO...

Find the location of each place you've traveled to while reading this book.

1. **The Federal Building:** 50 United Nations Plaza, San Francisco

2. **The Cathedral of Christ the Savior:** Moscow, Russia

3. **Ferguson:** Missouri

4. **Sydney Harbour Bridge:** Sydney, Australia

5. **Sidi Bouzid:** Tunisia

6. **Riyadh:** Saudi Arabia

7. **Stonewall Inn:** New York City, New York

8. **Marjory Stoneman Douglas High School:** Parkland, Florida

GLOSSARY

annexed (an-EKSD): took control of a country or territory by force

autocratic (aw-toh-KRA-tik): a person who rules with absolute power

avant-garde (ah-VANT-gard): new and unusual or experimental ideas, especially in the arts

delegation (del-i-GAY-shuhn): a group of people who represent an organization at meetings

federal (FED-ur-uhl): in a country with a federal government, such as the United States, several states are controlled by one power or central authority. However, each state also has its own government and can make its own laws

genocide (gen-ne-side): the deliberate killing of a large number of people from a particular nation or ethnic group with the aim of destroying that nation or group

LGBTQ+ (ell-gee-bee-tee-queue-pluhs): lesbian, gay, bisexual, transgender, and queer/questioning. 'Plus' encompasses any sexual orientations or gender identities that do not correspond to heterosexual norms

patriarch (PAY-tree-ahrk): head of the Eastern Orthodox Church

protesters (PROH-test-urs): people who make a demonstration or statement against something

provocative (proh-VAK-i-tiv): tending to provoke or purposely excite

reconciliation (REK-uhn-sill-ee-AYE-shuhn): the restoration of friendly relations

taboos (ta-BOO): a subject that may offend or upset people

INDEX

TEXT-DEPENDENT QUESTIONS

1. Name five styles of protest.

2. Name five issues that have had significant protest movements.

3. Which was the last country in the world to allow women to drive? What was the basis of the ban and when was it lifted?

4. What tradition did the Stonewall Uprising begin?

5. How long did the Section 504 protesters occupy the HEW offices in San Francisco? What were their demands?

EXTENSION ACTIVITY

What is an issue you care about? Draft an email to your local senator or congressperson, or the White House, about what the issue is and why it is important to you. Don't forget to do your research.

BIBLIOGRAPHY

Carter, David. *Stonewall: The Riots That Sparked the Gay Revolution.* St, Martin's Griffin, 2004.

Chenoweth, Erica and Maria J. Stephan. *Why Civil Resistance Works: The Strategic Logic of Nonviolent Conflict.* Columbia University Press, 2011.

Engler, Mark and Paul Engler. *This is an Uprising: How Nonviolent Revolt is Shaping the Twenty-First Century.* Bold Type Books, 2017.

Gillion, Daniel Q. *The Loud Minority: Why Protests Matter in American Democracy.* Princeton University Press, 2020.

Hasak-Lowy, Todd. *We Are Power: How Non-Violent Activism Changes the World.* Abrams Books for Young Readers, 2020.

Long, Michael G. Kids on the March: *15 Stories of Speaking Out, Protesting and Fighting for Justice.* Algonquin, 2021.

Paul, Caroline. *You Are Mighty.* Bloomsbury Publishing, 2018.

Perry, Lewis. *Civil Disobedience: An American Tradition.* Yale University Press, 2013.

Sharp, Gene. *Waging Nonviolent Struggle: 20th Century Practice and 21st Century Potential.* Extending Horizons Books, 2005.

Jen Breach (pronouns: they/them) is queer and nonbinary. Jen grew up in a tiny town in rural Australia with three older brothers, two parents, and one pet duck. Jen has worked as an archaeologist, a librarian, an editor, a florist, a barista, a bagel-baker, a code-breaker, a ticket-taker, and a trouble-maker. The best job they ever had was as a writer, which they do now in Philadelphia, PA. They have participated in a number of monumental demonstrations, including Black Lives Matter demonstrations in NYC, Boston, and Philly, Pride Parades, the Women's March, and the Melbourne Reconciliation Walk in 2000.

www.rourkeeducationalmedia.com

PHOTO CREDITS ©: Cover: Omer Messinger/Sipa USA/Newscom; Cover: Talaj / Shutterstock.com; Cover: Christopher Penler / Shutterstock.com; Cover: Rudy Balasko/ Shutterstock.com; Cover: an Witlen / Rmv/ZUMA Press/Newscom; Cover: Andrey_Kuzmin/ Shutterstock.com; All Pages: Andrey_Kuzmin/ Shutterstock.com; Page 1: LindoShots/ Shutterstock.com; Page 3: MrsWilkins/ Getty Images; Page 4: Leonid Andronov/ Shutterstock.com; Page 4: Anastasia Averina/ Shutterstock.com; Page 4: ucpage/ Shutterstock.com; Page 4: PJ_nice/ Shutterstock.com; Page 5: Mark Kolpakov/ Getty Images; Page 5: VDB Photos/ Shutterstock.com; Page 6: JOHN JERNEGAN /HO/Newscom; Page 8: Prostock-studio/ Shutterstock.com; Page 9: Ron Sachs/CNP/AdMedia/Newscom; Page 9: Benjamin E. "Gene" Forte / CNP / SplashNews/Newscom; Page 10: Alexei Nikolsky/TASS/Newscom; Page 10: Triff/ Shutterstock.com; Page 10: Vyacheslav Prokofyev/ZUMAPRESS/Newscom; Page 12: Yui Mok/ZUMA Press/Newscom/ Shutterstock.com; Page 12: Vector Icon Flat/ Shutterstock.com; Page 13: GRIGORY DUKOR/REUTERS/Newscom; Page 14: MAXIM SHEMETOV/REUTERS/Newscom; Page 14: Korotayev Artyom/Itar-Tass/ABACA/Newscom; Page 15: DONOT6_STUDIO / Shutterstock.com; Page 16: a katz / Shutterstock.com; Page 16: Gabriele Holtermann-Gorden/Sipa/Newscom; Page 17: Robert Cohen/TNS/Newscom; Page 18: RICK WILKING/REUTERS/Newscom; Page 19: Kristoffer Tripplaar/CNP/AdMedia/Newscom; Page 20: BILL GREENBLATT/UPI/Newscom; Page 20: RICK WILKING/REUTERS/Newscom; Page 21: Laurie Skrivan/ZUMA Press/Newscom; Page 23: Rudy Balasko/ Shutterstock.com; Page 23: MICK TSIKAS/REUTERS/Newscom; Page 23: PomInOz / Shutterstock.com; Page 24: MICK TSIKAS/REUTERS/Newscom; Page 24: ANDREW SHEARGOLD/REUTERS/Newscom; Page 24: Godong/ robertharding/Newscom; Page 24: TRACEY NEARMY/REUTERS/Newscom; Page 24: MICK TSIKAS/REUTERS/Newscom; Page 24: National Library of Australia/ PICRYL; Page 25: David Wimsett/UPPA/Photoshot/Newscom; Page 25: DAVID GRAY/REUTERS/Newscom; Page 26: Valery Bareta/ Shutterstock.com; Page 27: Images de Tunisie/Abaca/Newscom; Page 27: Images de Tunisie; Page 28: MAKOUKA/SIPA/Newscom; Page 29: Zoubeir Souissi/REUTERS/Newscom; Page 29: Pyty/ Shutterstock.com; Page 29: Pyty/ Shutterstock.com; Page 30: mosab ibra / Shutterstock.com; Page 31: FAHAD SHADEED/REUTERS/Newscom; Page 32: Gehad Hamdy/dpa/picture-alliance/Newscom; Page 33: CAITLIN OCHS/REUTERS/Newscom; Page 34: Vector FX/ Shutterstock.com; Page 34: Osugi / Shutterstock.com; Page 35: New York Public Library/ PICRYL; Page 36: ampueroleonardo/ Getty Images; Page 37: JEENAH MOON/REUTERS/Newscom; Page 37: Warren Eisenberg / Shutterstock.com; Page 37: Christopher Penler / Shutterstock.com; Page 38: Gabriele Holtermann-Gorden/Sipa/Newscom; Page 38: Jennifer Graylock/ZUMA Press/Newscom; Page 39: Richard B. Levine/Newscom; Page 40: Mike Stocker/TNS/Newscom; Page 40: Erin Scott/ZUMA Press/Newscom; Page 41: an Witlen / Rmv/ZUMA Press/Newscom; Page 42: Michael Nigro/ZUMA Press/Newscom; Page 42: Jeff Malet Photography/Newscom; Page 43: Carlos Bernate/ZUMA Press/Newscom; Page 44: Juliann/ Shutterstock.com

Library of Congress PCN Data

Places of Protest / Jen Breach
(Travel to...)
 ISBN 978-1-73165-184-6 (hard cover)
 ISBN 978-1-73165-229-4 (soft cover)
 Library of Congress Control Number: 2021944581

 ISBN 978-1-73165-199-0 (e-Book)
 ISBN 978-1-73165-214-0 (e-Pub)

Rourke Educational Media
Printed in the United States of America
02-09422119570

Edited by: **Hailey Scragg**
Cover and interior design by: **Joshua Janes**